Delmar the Dinky and the Animal Circus

Written by **Pat Danna**
Illustrated by **Pardeep Mehra**

In memory of my parents,
Frank and Catherine Danna

Copyright © 2022

All Rights Reserved. No part of this publication may be reproduced, stored in a retrieval system, or transmitted in any form by any means electronic, mechanical, photocopying, recording, or otherwise without the prior written permission of the publisher.

Illustrations by Pardeep Mehra
Cover & Layout by Praise Saflor

Publisher's Cataloging-in-Publication data

Names: Danna, Pat, author. | Mehra, Pardeep, illustrator.
Title: Delmar the Dinky and the animal circus / by Pat Danna; illustrated by Pardeep Mehra.
Series: Delmar the Dinky
Description: St. Louis, MO: Pat Danna, 2022. | Summary: A little trolley, called a dinky, rescues zookeeper Carl Hagenbeck's stranded circus animals on their way to the 1904 World's Fair in St. Louis.
Identifiers: LCCN: 2022905409 | ISBN: 978-1-7359960-4-2 (hardcover) | 978-1-7359960-3-5 (paperback) | 978-1-7359960-5-9 (ebook)
Subjects: LCSH Louisiana Purchase Exposition (1904 : Saint Louis, Mo.)--Juvenile fiction. | Trolley cars--Juvenile fiction. | Street railroads--Missouri--Saint Louis--Juvenile fiction. | Circus animals--Juvenile fiction. | BISAC JUVENILE FICTION / Historical / United States / 20th Century | JUVENILE FICTION /Readers / Beginner | JUVENILE FICTION / Social Themes / Self-Esteem & Self-Reliance | JUVENILE FICTION /Transportation / Railroads & Trains | JUVENILE FICTION / Animals / Zoo | JUVENILE FICTION / Performing Arts / Circus
Classification: LCC PZ7.1.D313 Del 2022 | DDC [E]--dc23

Hagenbeck's Animal Circus

Carl Hagenbeck (1844-1913) was a German animal trainer who collected wild animals for exhibitions. His animals were kept in open-air zoos without bars, very much like living in their natural habitat. He believed in the humane treatment of animals by showing you could train animals without unnecessary cruelty or beatings.

Hagenbeck's Zoological Paradise and Animal Circus was one of the most popular attractions at the 1904 World's Fair in St. Louis. Admission was ten cents to enter the exhibit to see open-air displays of wild animals. For an additional fee, fairgoers could see animal shows in a 3,000-seat theater.

Courtesy of the Missouri Historical Society

Delmar was a small trolley but ready to help anytime he was needed. "I'm strong enough to carry passengers, and I can move trains around the rail yard."

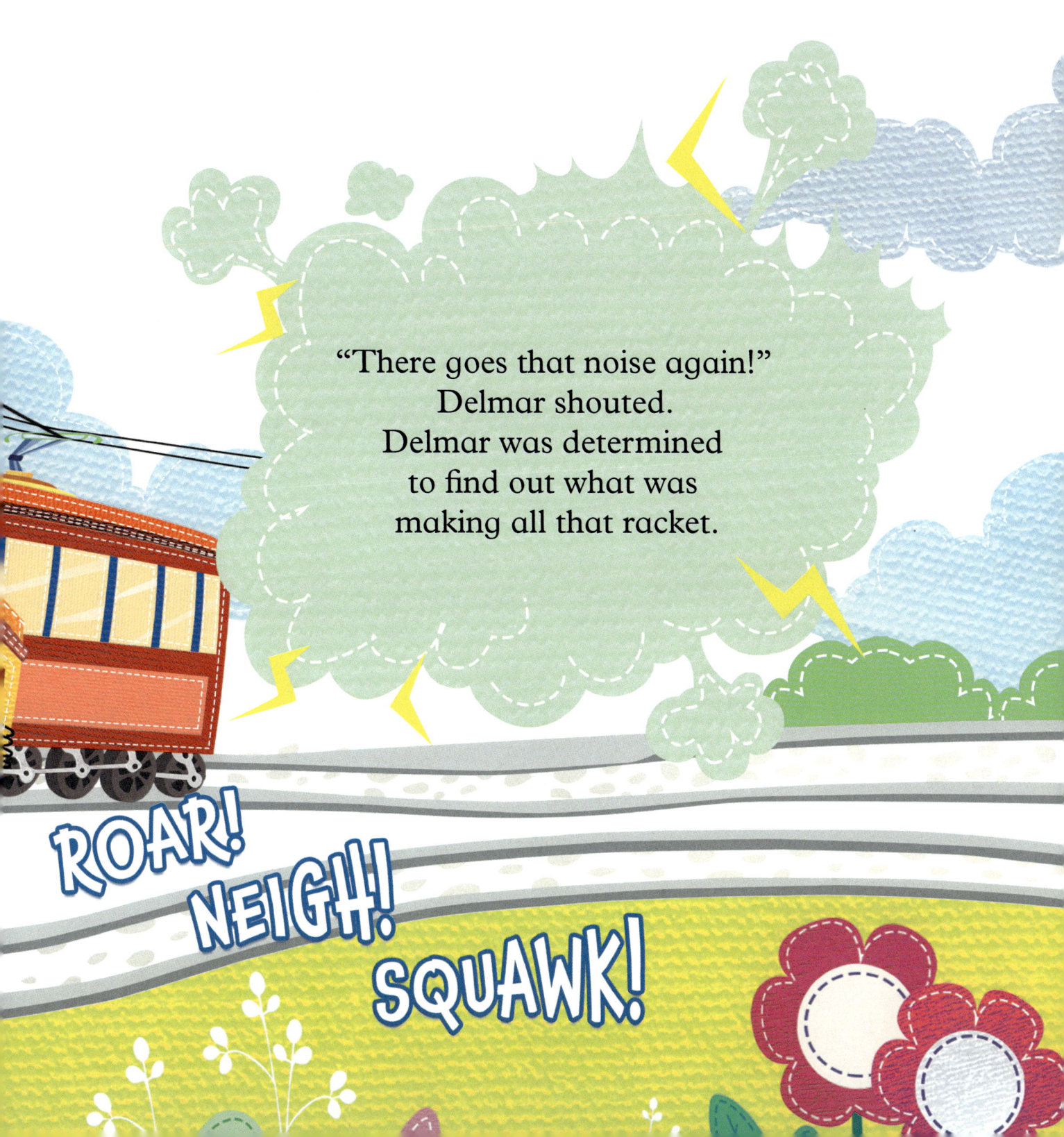

Just then, Delmar saw Conductor Noss.

"Oh no!" said the conductor. "Mr. Hagenbeck's circus animals are stuffed in a railcar. Where's the locomotive to pull their car to the fair?"

Mr. Hagenbeck's Animal Circus was invited to perform at the 1904 World's Fair in St. Louis.

For the first time, lions, bears, ostriches, monkeys, zebras, llamas and elephants would be allowed to roam free in a natural setting, not kept in cages.

"Sorry, the locomotive is blocked by a fallen tree," said the switchman.

"I can help!" shouted Delmar. But no one heard him over the roar of trains in the rail yard.

The conductor noticed a boxcar sitting on the side track. "Load the animals into the boxcar and get them to the fair."

"Sorry," said the switchman.
"The boxcar is full of luggage and mail."

"What do we do now?" asked Conductor Noss. "Maybe we should try the flatbed car."

Delmar nudged closer.
"Here I am! I can take some of the animals!" he shouted. Still, no one heard him.

The llama pranced around…
The tortoise moved so, so slowly…
But the ostrich broke loose and ran away!

"Catch that ostrich!" said the conductor. The animal trainer chased the big bird pecking grain from the hopper car.

"Oh dear, the flatbed car won't work.
It has no sides!" said the switchman.
The little dinky wasn't giving up.
He just had to get Conductor Noss's attention.
He dinged his bell...
flashed his headlight...
and revved his engine.

"Look, there's the dinky!" said the conductor.

"The dinky's too small," said the switchman. "Animals won't fit in the dinky!"

"He took passengers to the fair," said the conductor. " I'm sure he can take Mr. Hagenbeck's animals."

Delmar squeezed between two big trolleys and chugged up to the flatbed car.

Mr. Hagenbeck stepped aboard the dinky. Then the ostrich, bear, monkey, camel, and llama climbed the ramp. And the tortoise finally made it, but so…so…so slowly!

Delmar was so proud he helped the animals.

With his new animal friends, Delmar the Dinky arrived at the fairgrounds right on time.

CLICKETY CLACK! CLICKETY CLACK!

Did you enjoy reading
*Delmar The Dinky
And The Animal Circus*?

Thanks for joining *Delmar the Dinky* on his new adventure.

If you have a moment to spare, I would really appreciate a short review on the site where you bought my book.

Reviews make a huge difference to authors
and are greatly appreciated.

You might enjoy reading the first book in the series:

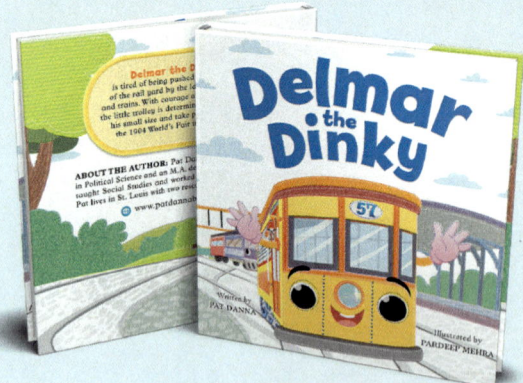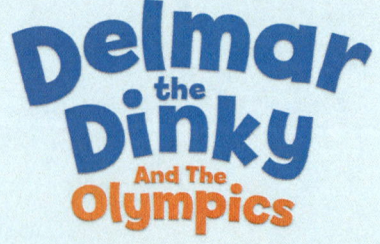

Coming soon!

Available in: e-book, paperback, hardcover
on Amazon or your local bookstore.

www.patdannabooks.com

Made in the USA
Middletown, DE
15 October 2022